WALKS AROUND Matlock

10 WALKS UNDER 6 MILES

DALESMAN

Dalesman Publishing Company Ltd
Stable Courtyard, Broughton Hall,
Skipton, North Yorkshire BD23 3AE

First Edition 1998

A British Library Cataloguing in Publication record
is available for this book

ISBN 1 85568 148 X

Printed by Amadeus Press, Huddersfield

Contents

Introduction

The ten walks in this book are all close to Matlock and Matlock Bath. They are designed for the casual walker, the walker with time to spare and for those with young families where speed and distance are not possible. The walks take in some of the finest countryside round Matlock, the limestone gorges and dales, the gritstone tors and moors. The descriptions and the accompanying maps will enable you to undertake the walks safely. However, you are strongly advised to obtain a copy of the OS Outdoor Leisure Map No. 24: The White Peak. This covers all but a few yards of the walks in this book and is a work of art in its own right.

None of the walks involve serious climbing, but Matlock and its environs are not for those who like flat walks, though the Cromford canal is the exception. Good footwear is essential and even on the best of days the weather can let you down. A waterproof is a wise precaution. One or two of the walks visit the limestone or gritstone outcrops where children of all ages can enjoy scrambling about and getting the feel of hard rock in their hands and under their feet. Robin Hood's Stride, Black Rocks and Harboro' Rocks are the best examples, but there are others. Few dads will be able to resist the temptation to "look after the kids" in such circumstances.

The Matlock area has a fine network of footpaths and bridleways, most of which are easy to follow. In the area covered by this book, the authority responsible for their repair and maintenance is Derbyshire County Council, with assistance from the Derbyshire Dales District Council, and the Peak National Park. Please report any difficulties to one or other of these bodies. All the walks in this book can be reached by public transport. There is information aplenty from the Derbyshire Busline on 01332 292200, or from the tourist information centre in Matlock Bath on 01629 55082.

Most of the walks pass places of refreshment and these are indicated in the text. Most pubs serve food and allow children inside if food is being purchased. In the larger villages there is usually a shop and even in the countryside you will come across the ubiquitous ice cream van. Nevertheless, a rucksack with food and drinks is a wise precaution. Please remember that the countryside is a working environment, someone else's livelihood. You will not endear yourself to the locals by letting dogs or children run riot, by dropping litter, by leaving gates open or damaging stiles and walls. Take nothing but photographs, leave nothing but footprints.

Enjoy your walking.

Ashover, Overton and Milltown

Length of walk: 3 miles.
Start/finish: The Crispin Inn, Ashover. Monday to Saturday bus service from Chesterfield and Matlock. Car parking by the village hall.
Terrain: Easy footpaths with few steep or rough stretches.

From the Crispin, where the inn sign is worth study, go over the road and down the narrow track beside the Institute. There is an inscription over the door in both English and Latin, though the two don't mean the same. 'Train a child in the way he should go and when he is old he will not depart from it' is the English version.

Continue along the track, passing the playing fields on the left and resisting the temptation to stop and watch the regular cricket matches. The path passes the cricket pavilion and goes through a stile, following a wall on the left. On the left, on top of the hill is the unmistakable shape of the Fabrick rock, whilst in the valley lie the remains of Eastwood Hall, one of the victims of the Civil War. Continue straight ahead through a series of fields, noting the looming bulk of Cocking Tor to the right. A glance at the field walls will reveal that they are a mixture of limestone and gritstone, for Ashover is a microcosm of Derbyshire. Here you are on the limestone, but Eastwood Hall lies on the shale and the Fabrick is a gritstone outcrop.

Soon the path follows the left hand wall of the field round to the right. The path comes close to a steep drop on the right, before swinging left by a fence. On the right the land falls away into a former fluorspar pit, now disused and slowly being filled. Pass through a stile into an area of woodland, with old workings on either side. Were it not for the trees, this would be a rocky ridge. The path soon drops to reach another stile at a T junction of paths. Turn right here, passing through a gate. The big pit is now close on the right and the path is

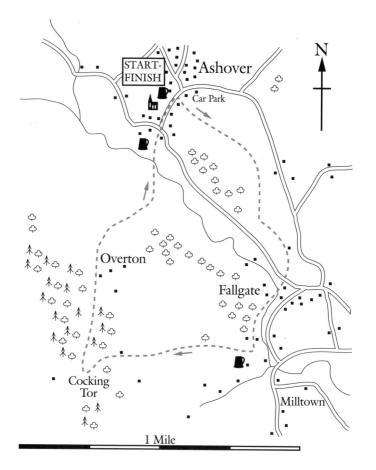

diverted away from the edge. Despite the misleading waymark, keep close to the fence on the right, quickly passing the concrete slabs that once formed the floors of buildings. It is worth looking into the pit, though not too closely. The remains of old mine workings can be seen in the quarry walls. The bottom of the pit is frequently filled by a deep blue pool.

The path soon leaves this area of industrial despoilation and, passing a bungalow on the left, drops down a flight of steps onto the road. Take care here as there is no footway or verge. Go left and then turn right just past

Greenbank Cottage. Go down the drive and then down a narrow path left of the garage. This can be overgrown, but leads downhill, passing over a stone slab bridge, before emerging on the road again close to a junction.

To the right, just over the river, lay the former Ashover Light Railway. The station buildings remain just to the left. Don't venture any further, but go along the road, beside the River Amber, and turn right at the next footpath sign. Cross the river and turn left, following a narrow path along the riverbank, through the trees. Soon the path swings right, keeping beside the boundary fence and leaving the riverbank. At the T junction turn right, soon descending a couple of steps to cross the former railway line again. The path rises away from the railway, keeping company with the Milltown washery fence on the right and passing the remains of an old lead mine on the left. Do not explore too closely, for the trees and brambles obscure a shaft.

Pass through a stile into fields and follow the path to a rough lane. The lane leads unerringly towards Cocking Tor which can be seen ahead. On either side are the overgrown remains of old workings, now indistinguishable from any other woodland that has been let run riot. As the Tor is approached the landscape becomes more open. Bear left at the junction of tracks and follow the rough lane up, past the old washery, to the cottages. Just beyond the cottages, the path climbs away up the hillside through the scrub. This tumbled land was the site of the great Gregory Mine, long closed. Note the chimney on the left. Paths scramble up through the hillocks, but keep close to the right hand side if possible, until an obvious crossing track is reached. Here go right, into the trees.

An obvious though muddy path runs through the trees, soon passing a spring on the left and giving views down to Overton on the right. Where Overton Hall comes into view the track becomes paved with big gritstone slabs, known as causey stones, sure signs of heavy ancient use.

Follow the track to a cross roads and go straight across. A narrow lane climbs slightly to reach the crest of the limestone again. At the T junction, by the cattle grid, there is a fine view over Ashover. Go through the stile and descend the steep field on the paved path, soon reaching a deep cut hollow-way. At the bottom of the hill the hollow-way levels out and becomes a hedged track, swinging left to run alongside the former railway again. The remains of Salters Lane station can just be discerned on the right, a raised area that was once the platform. The track crosses the railway and then the Amber on a fine packhorse bridge, before a last steep climb, up to the village. Salters Lane emerges on the road beside the Red Lion. A quick left and right takes you back to the church, the shop selling ice creams and the Crispin.

Black Rocks and Cromford Moor

Length of walk: 4 miles.
Start/finish: Black Rocks car park, just off the Cromford-Wirksworth road. Daily bus service from Matlock passes the site.
Terrain: Easy going on High Peak Trail, tracks and field paths. Little climbing, but a grand optional scramble, a visit to some coral reefs and a narrow gauge railway.

From the Black Rocks visitor centre go on to the High Peak Trail and turn left. The Trail was once a railway line, opened in 1830 and closed in the late 1960s. It was built using canal technology, with long level stretches, punctuated with steep inclines. It is hard to imagine that a railway ran here now. Pass Railway Slab Rock on the left, noting the inscribed initials, CHR, the Cromford and Highpeak Railway. Adventurous types will want to have a go at climbing the slab. Continue along the Trail admiring the superb view to the left, over Riber and Matlock Gorge. This is by far the most scenic part of the Trail.

Soon the Trail reaches the top of Sheep-pasture incline. The pond provided water for the winding engine and the gaunt engine house is a reminder of railway days. Formerly there was an engine shed here and waggons were attached to the wire rope prior to being lowered down the incline to the canal wharf far below. Begin the descent of the incline, soon passing through a rock cutting and reaching a signpost pointing to Whatstandwell. Leave the Trail at this point and follow the path down to a track, there turning right. Follow the track steadily up through woodland. At the edge of the wood the track turns sharp right and shortly afterwards, at a gate and stile, turn sharp left.

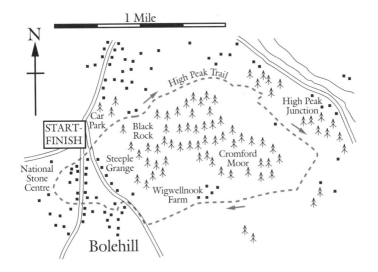

Follow this delightful green lane, with a sudden and unexpected view of Crich Stand and church to the left. Bole Hill television mast is to the right. The lane is the last resting place of some interesting old farm machinery, including a combined harvester and a horse dray. The latter is at least 75 years old. See how many other pieces you can spot and identify. Pass the barn on the right and then a caravan site on the left, soon reaching a corrugated metal barn, on the left. Opposite this there is a waymarked stile. Turn right here, leaving the lane. Keep alongside the wall on the left through a couple of fields, with a view left to Crich. At the end of the second field there is a stile on the left and then another immediately to the right.

These are waymarked. At this point the path forks. Bear right, heading up the middle of the field, following the tractor ruts, to the right hand stile and gateway. Continue straight ahead, with Alport Hill masts coming into view to the left and a good view back when you reach the next stile and gate. The obvious path continues ahead through an area of scrub and gorse, soon reaching a track. The track is followed past Wigwellnook Farm. Look out for the lead mine spoil heap on the left and the fine beehive structure covering the shaft. Soon the track joins the road and here you turn right. There is a fine view over Middleton and Wirksworth.

Follow the road downhill for about 350 yards, passing a footpath sign on the right. Now look out for a stile on the left. A tarred path descends steeply past a terrace of houses, soon coming into the area known as The Lanes. The path joins a driveway and soon reaches a T junction where you turn right. Follow the narrow lane past the houses and cottages, descending to an awkward road junction. Go right here and then immediately left, near the sign indicating that this is Nan Gell's Hill.

At the main road, by the war memorial, go right and then left, along an unmarked track near the bus stop, which leads into the National Stone Centre. On either side are the limestone knolls that were once coral reefs. Information boards describe the site. The path passes the visitor centre on the left. This is worth a visit and serves refreshments. Just before the bridge, turn right and ascend to the High Peak Trail. Turn right at the top, following the signs to Black Rocks and the Light Railway. After about 300 yards the Trail passes the narrow gauge railway station at Steeplehouse. This little line operates on summer weekends along the track of the old Killers Branch and uses old mining and quarrying rolling stock.

Continue along the Trail, crossing the Cromford-Wirksworth road on a superb stone embankment and bridge. Again there is a grand view to the left to Cromford and Matlock, whilst ahead towers the gritstone outcrop of Black Rocks. Soon Black Rocks picnic site is reached and with it the information centre, ice cream van and the end of the walk. The energetic amongst you will probably wish to scale the Black Rocks, if only for the view and to see if you can find the rare fossil in the gritstone.

Brassington and Harboro' Rocks

Length of walk: 4¹/₂ miles from Miners Arms ; 5 miles from Sheepwash
Start/finish: Carsington Sheepwash car park (sparse bus service from Matlock and Wirksworth). Parking at Sheepwash car park.
Terrain: Mainly easy going, on good paths, but a grand scrambly section at Harbro' Rocks and a steep descent into Carsington.

Leave the car park by the footpath signed to the Bird Hide. Ignore the next sign to the hide and carry straight on, descending to water level and skirting a narrow arm of the reservoir. Soon the road is reached. Cross and follow the waymarked Carsington circular walk up a narrow hedged track. The track becomes a tarred lane at Wash Farm. At the T junction bear right, descending into Carsington village close to the back of the Miners Arms. Turn left, following the lane to the main road, passing the village green.

At the main road, continue straight ahead, but where the road swings left, go up the lane, marked No Through Road. Climb steadily, soon revealing a view over Carsington Water. Once past the last house, the lane degenerates into a track and soon enters fields. The path is signed to Brassington and runs round the base of Carsington Pasture, which rises steeply to the right. An obvious terraced path swings round the hillside. Beyond a gate and stile the track forks. Bear right, up the hillside, heading for a narrow V shaped cutting. All around are the remains of old lead mines.

Climb through the cutting and onto the top of the hill. Pass through a derelict wall and then through a gap in the wall ahead. The view ahead is towards Parwich and Tissington, with tree topped Moot Low on the horizon. Descend to a stile just to the left of a barn. Cross a rough track onto open pastureland again. A track bears away to the left and then curls round to the right, tending uphill to the remains of Nickalum Mine. As you near the mine a waymark sign directs you left, skirting round the grassed spoil banks. Pass through a cutting and Brassington comes into view below. The path runs between a mass of former lead mines, descending steadily to a stile near a thorn tree. Follow the wall on the left until a stile is reached. Go left, descending the field, soon crossing another stile on the right. Follow the path through a couple more fields to emerge in Brassington via a farm access.

Turn right at the road and follow it up, through the village for about 300 yards. At a road junction, where the main road carries straight on, turn right, up a narrow lane. Continue up the lane with outcrops of limestone on either side, until the road

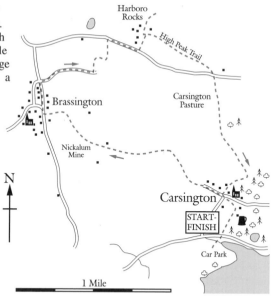

comes to a sudden stop. Ahead lie the results of silica sand mining, but a path diverges to the left, climbing round the old workings, through fields. As you top the rise, Harboro' Rocks can be seen ahead, offering a good scramble. The path hugs the boundary of the silica workings and soon reaches Manystones Lane. Turn right and follow the road for about 300 yards, taking care as there is no footpath. Pass the entrance to Harboro' Works and at the footpath sign go left, soon reaching the High Peak Trail. Go straight across the Trail and make your way to the top of Harboro' Rocks.

Return to the Trail and turn left. Soon, just before the gate across the Trail, by Viaton works, take the signed path to the right. Cross the little field and the road to enter Carsington Pasture once more. The path runs alongside the wall, with the remains of a windmill seen to the left. Keep by the wall onto the top of the Pasture. Suddenly there is a tremendous view over Carsington Water. Pass the rock formation known as the King's Chair, on the left, and follow the wall to the wood before turning right and descending to Carsington. The path is waymarked through a gate, into a back garden, down a flight of steps onto a lane which emerges in the village. Turn left to reach the Miners Arms. For Sheepwash car park, bear right before the pub and retrace your steps past Wash Farm, over the by-pass and back by the reservoir.

Crich and Cromford Canal

Length of walk: 4½ miles.
Start/finish: Crich market place. Daily bus service from Matlock.
Limited street parking in village.
**Terrain: Easy going on good paths. One lengthy ascent, but a flat
section beside the canal.**

Leave the market place via Sandy Lane, to the right of the Baptist chapel.
Continue up the lane, soon passing the reading rooms on the left. Then look
out for a stile, just to the left of a bungalow. This leads onto The Tors. This
is a gritstone edge from which there are wide views east and west.
Hardwick Hall and Bolsover Castle can be seen to the left. Stroll along the
top of The Tors, which is an old quarry working, until the path drops sharply
to reach Chadwick Nick. The Crich Mineral Railway, built by Stephenson in
1841, used to cross the road on the level about 100 yards to the left.

Turn right at the road and pass through the Nick, taking care as there is
neither footway nor verge. Follow the road down to the right hand bend and
there pass through a stile on the left. Follow the left hand wall through the
fields to the lip of the Derwent valley. There are good views across to
Shining Cliff Woods and Alderwasley. Go left along the edge of the valley,
soon entering Crich Chase Wood. This is a grand area of mixed deciduous
woodland, through which the obvious path runs, twisting and turning
between the trees, until an open area is reached with a ruined barn on the
left. The path bears right, re-entering woodland. Where the path forks, bear
left, descending to join another track and then bearing right, down a narrow
twisting hollow-way. This soon reaches open fields, where you bear right,
heading for a gate in the far left hand corner of the field. Pass through the
gate, over the canal bridge and turn right, along the towpath, soon passing
the remains of a wharf.

The next section is so deceptively easy that you could do it with your eyes
shut; not that this is advisable on a canal towpath. The canal was opened in
1793, the main traffic being coal and limestone. It passed into railway hands
in 1852 and by 1899 traffic at this end of the canal was down to a mere 1,000
tonnes of limestone and 3-4,000 tonnes of coal. This ceased with the
collapse of Butterley tunnel in 1900 and the canal was abandoned in 1944.

Now it is a nature reserve, managed by Derbyshire County Council.

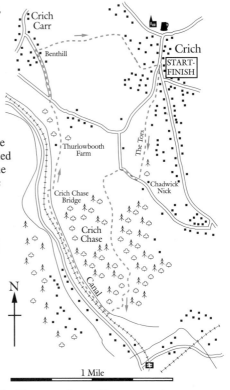

Follow the towpath for about a mile, to Crich Chase Bridge. Cross the canal here and then turn left, following a broad track through the wood. The track soon becomes a walled lane, which despite the 'Private' signs is a public footpath. Where the lane forks, keep right and go over a stile. Keep straight on, soon emerging from the woodland onto a road at Chasecliff, where there is a seat with fine views over the Derwent valley. Cross the road and go up the lane opposite, known as Shaw's Hill. Shaws Hill becomes Top Lane and dips slightly. Now look out for a narrow ginnel between houses on the right. If you reach an old pump you have gone too far. Turn right, up the ginnel, climbing steeply up a flight of steps, crossing a narrow walled lane and then ascending more steps before reaching the Benthill Farm access. Climb a few more steps, then the gradient eases, you enter fields and Crich Stand can be seen to the left.

Go straight on through the fields, with the spire of Crich church coming into view and forming a good marker. Soon the top of the hill is reached and the path continues ahead, making for the church. A track crosses the path. To visit the National Tramway Museum, turn left here, retracing your steps to this point afterwards. Otherwise, turn right along the track, which soon reaches houses and becomes a narrow road called Wheatsheaf Lane. Bear right where Jeffreys Lane joins, passing the bridge that was part of Stephenson's railway. At the next road junction, go left for the Market Place.

14

Cromford and Lea Mills

Length of walk: 4 miles.
Start/finish: Cromford railway station (daily trains from Matlock).
Parking at the station.
Terrain: Very easy, half on towpath, the rest on good field paths and tracks. No serious climbing. Probably the flattest walk in this book.

Having admired the ornate little station, now sadly decaying, go down the approach road and turn right at the bottom. Follow the road past the Starkholmes junction and the access to Willersley Castle before bearing left to cross the ancient bridge over the Derwent. This medieval bridge still retains its pointed arches on the downstream side. It also serves as the finish of the annual Boxing Day raft race. Continue along the road for a few more minutes, passing the fishing temple on the left, before turning left into the canal wharf, now a picnic site and car park owned by Derbyshire County Council. The wharf still boasts the full range of buildings and is lovely.

Follow the towpath for a delightfully easy and pleasant mile. The canal runs above the meadowland, on a shelf cut into the hillside. Look out for the sluice gates that control the water level and see if you can spot the slots for the stop planks under the bridge. These enable sections of the canal to be drained whilst still retaining water in the remainder.

Soon the railway comes alongside and the canal and railway run through a thickly wooded area, before reaching Highpeak Junction. Here the canal made contact with the Cromford and High Peak Railway, opened in 1830 and closed in the late 1960s. The original intention had been to build a canal to connect the Cromford Canal to the Peak Forest Canal at Whaley Bridge, but on the advice of the engineer, Jessop, a partner in the Butterley ironworks, a railway was built instead. The railway workshops and transhipment sheds still exist and are worth a visit, if only for refreshments.

Continuing along the towpath, you soon pass Leawood Pump House, which was built to raise water from the Derwent into the canal. This fine structure still contains the pumping engine which is operated for visitors. Just beyond the pump house the canal crosses the Derwent on an aqueduct. This caused

15

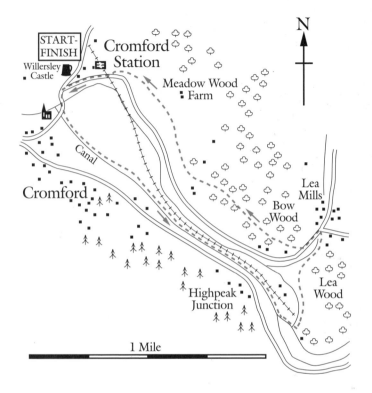

the engineer considerable heartache during construction as it collapsed and he had to repair it at his own expense. At the far end of the aqueduct there is a set of stop planks and a small swing bridge. Do not cross, but turn left along the derelict Leawood Arm. This branch canal served Leawood Mills. It is a substantial construction with stone retaining walls into the meadows and on the hillside. The towpath crosses the railway between Leawood Tunnel mouth and the girder bridge over the Derwent. Beyond the railway the canal is no longer in water, but the towpath is still well used.

Soon the old wharf is reached, with the buildings now converted to a private house. Embedded in the wharf are the circular remains of a crane, used for hoisting goods into and out of the boats. A wide track now continues ahead, forking by a stone house. Bear left here, descending to the road at Lea Mills, the mills being just to the right at this point.

Turn left along the road and cross the bridge which spans the Lea Brook. Cross the road and go through a stile/gate on the right. Do not follow the track to Splash Farm. A lovely woodland walk now follows, through Bow Wood, now in the ownership of the Woodland Trust. After the short initial climb the path wanders easily through the wood. Pass under a wonderfully bowed beech tree, which offers enticing prospects for adventurous pioneers. Ignore turnings to right and left, even if they are waymarked, and continue along the terraced path until it emerges from the wood into a walled track.

This runs past Sunnybank House to join a narrow lane. Turn left and follow the lane downhill for about 300 yards, with good views over Cromford Meadows, which will be especially interesting to rugby fans. Where the electricity line crosses the lane, go through a stile on the right and strike diagonally left across the field, negotiating two muddy patches in the process. The exit stile is well hidden in the far corner, but the path is obvious. In the next field the grassy path runs on a terrace past a spring and trough before passing through a gateway and climbing, following what passes for a wall and hedge. The path levels out and continues along a terrace to a stile into End Wood.

In the wood the path twists and turns through the trees, sometimes muddily, but always distinct. On emerging from the trees at a stile, an obvious path carries on across the field, but instead, turn left here and make your way down by the side of the field, soon picking up a clear but muddy path. This is not as shown on the OS map. The path continues steeply downhill through rough grass and scrub before emerging on the Cromford-Lea road at a stile. Go right, along the footway, passing under the railway bridge. There are steps up to the station just beyond the bridge.

Lumsdale and the Pine Ridge

Length of walk: 2 miles.
Start/finish: Bus stop on Chesterfield Road at the end of Lumsdale.
Parking in lay-by in Lumsdale Road opposite Highfields School.
Terrain: Mainly obvious paths and tracks through woods and fields.
Short steep climb on steps.

From the bus stop at Lumsdale on the Chesterfield Road, go down Lumsdale Road, passing Slacks garage on the left and Highfields School on the right. Just beyond the lay-by go left, over the footbridge spanning Bentley Brook. Follow the embankment, skirting an old dam, one of many in this valley. The dam is now dry and overgrown with trees. The curious diggings on the right amongst the undergrowth are the antics of 'bottle diggers', for this patch of land was once a waste tip.

At a T junction, turn left and continue uphill, with an excellent view to the right towards Riber and Masson. At the next junction bear right along a reasonably level, but rough path. Despite its natural appearance, this was once a quarry and you are making your way across the old waste tips, now overgrown with pines, birch and oak trees and covered with bilberry and heather. As the path twists and turns amongst the rocks and trees there are superb views to the right over Matlock Dale and up the Derwent valley towards Rowsley.

The path swings sharp left, drops briefly and steeply before climbing again and turning right to resume its course along the hillside. Another descent and the path forks. Keep right, following the twisting path through the trees until it forks again. Bear left and thus reach a track. Here the walk comes out into the open again with a grand view over to Tansley and Riber, which is just overtopped by Bole Hill television mast.

Turn left along the track which soon becomes a tarred road, descending steeply past Oaksedge Farm towards Tansley. Follow the road down to the bottom of the hill. If there is a demand for refreshment, then continue ahead,

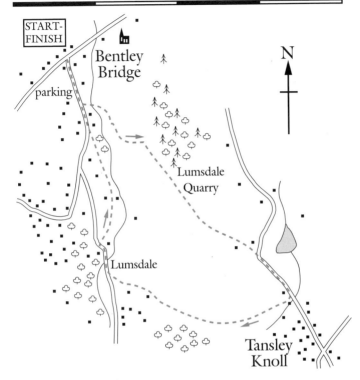

up into Tansley and the Gate Inn, otherwise turn right, just before the bridge. The track is signed to Lumsdale and Matlock Bank. Follow the obvious track through three gates/stiles, ignoring turns to right or left. Once through the third stile continue alongside the wall on the right to a kissing gate. Follow the left hand fence across the field, which shows clear signs of ridge and furrow farming, to another stile, just to the right of the house. The path runs alongside the house, passing the garage and a huge spreading chestnut tree, before reaching open fields again. Descend the field, beside the right hand fence to a couple of stiles leading out onto a road. This is Lumsdale. The place-name Lum or Lumb means a steep sided wooded valley and this is certainly true in this case.

Turn right at the road, soon passing the first of a series of old ruined mills.

This complex was at its height in the late 18th century and is now in the care of the Arkwright Society. It is a fascinating example of what could be done using water power and the natural landform. Continue up the road to a gateway on the right, with an Arkwright Society notice beside it. Turn right here into the main mill complex. This is a concessionary path and can be closed at any time, but it is usually made freely available by the Society. Keep children firmly under control here, for although the whole place is a fascinating one for youngsters it can be dangerous, with some considerable drops and hidden crevices.

The path winds its way up the valley side on flights of steps, with the Bentley Brook roaring away to the right. There are glimpses of a waterfall and soon it is possible to take a path on the right to the foot of the fall, an impressive sight at any time but particularly when in spate. Continue upwards until the main mill ruins are reached and then pass through the doorway ahead. To the right is a huge fenced wheel pit. The water from the upper dams was used again and again in its journey down the valley.

Continue upwards through the ruins, soon nearing another waterfall, which is the overflow from the dam. The path now swings through another ruin, ascends a few more steps and reaches a delightful mill pond. Follow the path beside the pool to the cottages, then follow the track between the houses. These buildings used to be a lead smelter and some of the stones in the left hand wall show signs of having been part of the furnace.

Continue along the track, passing the remains of another dam on the right. The track soon forks, but keep straight ahead along the wider route, soon reaching yet another ruined dam. Just beyond this point the track joins a road, trailing in from the left. Notice the litter bin which for some inexplicable reason is labelled in Welsh and English! A short step along this quiet lane, passing a cottage on the right designed by Sir Joseph Paxton, soon brings you back to the school and the outward route. There is a little shop at the road end, which sells ice cream and soft drinks.

Masson and the Heights of Abraham

Length of walk: 4 miles.
Start/finish: Matlock railway station (car park adjacent).
Terrain: Obvious paths and tracks, but quite steep climbing and slippery when wet.

From the railway station go to the main road and turn right, up Snitterton Road, passing the florists on the left. Just past the florists, bear left up a narrow lane signposted as the Limestone Way. At Bridge Farm a flight of steps leads into fields. Walk up the obvious grassy groove. Half way up the field bear left at a waymarker post. A narrow, but distinct path cuts across the field to a stile, with grand views across the valley to Riber Castle and Matlock.

Continue through a couple more fields to a double stile where a track is joined and you turn left. Wind your way round the head of a little valley, with a sudden view ahead to the Victoria Tower on the Heights of Abraham. High Tor soon comes into view on the far side of the valley. Pass through a couple of stiles, soon reaching St. John's Road. Continue up the road, passing the chapel on the right. This was built in Victorian times by a local landowner, who fell out with the Rector of Matlock. Paradoxically the chapel now comes under the jurisdiction of the present Rector of Matlock.

At the road end, go to the right of the gateway, following signs to the Heights of Abraham. The path runs beside the wall on slippery limestone, soon reaching a stile and a wood. More slippery limestone follows; the path passing a farm on the left, thus reaching open hillside. Ahead is the Victoria Tower, whilst to the left is a fine view over the Matlock Gorge. Follow the waymarks up to the right, to a stile. Continue upwards on an obvious path, noting the curious conical metal structure on the left which covers a lead mine shaft. Masson hillside is riddled with shafts, so it pays not to stray too far from the paths. The path winds through hawthorn thickets, soon reaching a stile and gate, quite close to the tower. Follow the waymarked path upwards, crossing a track. This leads into the Heights of Abraham grounds from Masson Mine, a show cave. Continue upwards for a short way then go left at a waymarked stile, passing round the cleft which marks the entrance to the cavern.

The path crosses a track before entering the thick woodland fringing this side of the Matlock Gorge. Except in winter, there is no sign of Matlock Bath, though it is only just below. The path twists and twines through the trees, eventually passing through a thorn thicket before reaching an open area near Ember Farm. Bear right here, passing the farm on the right and joining Ember Lane.

There is a good view south, over Black Rocks and Alport to Crich. Follow the lane for about 200 yards, then turn right, just before a barn on your left. Pass through a stile into open fields and head towards the monolithic remaining stone of another stile. Bonsall can be seen below and to the left. Continue straight ahead, through a series of fields, passing a barn on the right. Then follow the left hand hedge down the field, before passing through a gap at the bottom corner and reaching a gate and stile. Go slightly left, then right, following the narrow walled lane which skirts round the back of Bonsall. This is an ancient packhorse route and has an alternative field path running parallel on the left in case the main route is too muddy. The lane descends slightly to a T junction. Turn right, beginning to climb again, soon reaching open fields. To the left is a grand view across the limestone plateau. At the top of the hill there is a gate and a well signposted stile. Go right here, cutting across the narrow field to pass between the two barns. Until recently this next stretch was a wide green lane, but the walls on the left have been destroyed.

An obvious path follows the old wall line to reach a stile into a track leading to the top of Masson Hill. Here a tremendous view opens up to the north, taking in Darley Dale and a long length of the Derwent valley. Go straight ahead, through another stile, then bear right. At the next stile go left, beginning the descent to Matlock, seen bird's eye fashion, below.

22

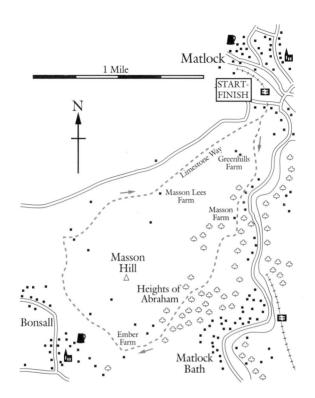

The clear path descends steadily, soon reaching Geoff's seat, a grand place to sit and admire the view. Go right here, then immediately bear left, through a signposted stile, descending again and soon reaching a stile just to the left of Masson Lees Farm. Go over the farm track and through another stile, descending beside the wall. Keep straight ahead, descending all the time, soon reaching a waymarked stile by a metal gate. Don't follow the track to the left, but keep straight on, alongside the wall on the right. The path runs almost straight, always beside the wall or hedge, but occasionally swopping from side to side. One such swop is easily missed, beside a gateway. The stile is well hidden in a thorn thicket.

A series of stiles and fields now follows until the path reaches the track leading to Greenhills Farm. Cross the track and go through the stile into the final field. Descend steeply, soon reaching the stile and steps by Bridge Farm. It is then but a short step back to the station.

Oker Hill and Wensley Dale

Length of walk: 5¹/₂ miles.
Start/finish: Square and Compass pub at Darley Bridge. Monday to Saturday bus service from Matlock (daily service to Whitworth Centre on A6, add ¹/₂ mile in each direction). Parking at Darley Bridge picnic site on B5057 or on the gated road to Oker, left beyond Darley Bridge. Terrain: The most difficult walk in the book for route finding. One steep ascent, some poetical associations and some grand views.

From the Square and Compass, go over the fine old bridge which spans the Derwent, noting the shape of the arches, round on the north side, whilst some of those on the south side are pointed. Once over the bridge, turn left along the 'gated road to Oker'. Almost at once, turn right, through a signposted stile. Bear left, on an obvious path, with Oker Hill in view ahead. Negotiate the mud guarded stile, go up the next field to reach a track, and turn left. Follow the track, with a good view left into Two Dales. Pass the houses on the left and continue ahead, through a gateway. Follow the waymarked path which bears right, heading uphill though a clump of gorse to a stile. The path wanders steadily upwards across the tumbled flanks of Oker Hill, passing through an area of hawthorn scrub, with one or two waymarks.

Soon the path emerges into the open with good views up and down the valley. Head for the curious spiked fence post. At the second of these, if you intend to scale Oker Hill, bear right, making for a waymarker post on top of the ridge. Here turn right and follow the obvious path up the ridge, until Will Shaw's tree is reached. This commemorates the parting of two brothers, who each planted a tree near this spot. The event is immortalised in one of Wordsworth's poems. The trig point on top of Oker Hill is only a stone's throw away along a delightful narrow ridge. The view from here is superb.

Retrace your steps to the waymarker post where you joined the ridge, turn left down the slope, then right on reaching the main path. Pass a stone lined spring known as Grace's Well, then go left through an awkward stile. Bear right through scrub into open fields. Slant left, down to a stile in the far corner, near the road junction. At the junction go left for 50 yards, then turn right, at a signpost, into fields again. Follow this path through a series of

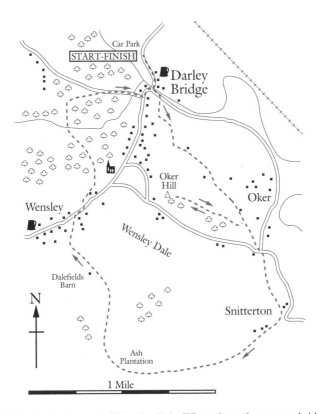

fields, into the bottom end of Wensley Dale. Where the path crosses a bridge, go straight on. Do not bear left along the more obvious track. At the far side of the field is a signpost. (To avoid the main climb and the more tricky navigation, it is possible to turn right here, following the signs to Wensley.)

Go straight on, through a small field, into a narrow ginnel between houses, to emerge on the road at Snitterton Bull Ring. Turn right, passing the bull ring. Keep right at the junction, leaving the 'main' road and following a narrow lane. Where this forks, keep right, skirting the grounds of Snitterton Hall, a fine Elizabethan mansion, unfortunately hidden.

Where the lane finishes, the path continues through a farmyard, curving left to a waymarked stile and gate, back into fields. A rough track continues beside the hedge up to a double gate, where there is a view of the hall.

Beyond the gate an overgrown hollow-way bears right. Follow this up to a waymarked gate. Keep left of the wall, through a field with obvious signs of lead mining, to a stile and gate.

The terraces in the next field are strip lynchets, the remains of early farming practice. Part way across this field a waymark indicates left, to a gap in the ruined wall. The next field is steep and pathless, but follow a terrace to the remains of an old mine. Skirt round to the right of the ruined building and then follow the fence on the right, up and through the scrub to locate a waymarked stile. Bear left in the next field, through scrubby thorns, to locate a stile in the top right hand corner. The path now enters Ash Plantation, a curious area of limestone boulders and old mine remains. The path soon emerges from the plantation and runs beside a wall on the right, with a grand view up the Derwent valley and over to Wensley. Descend into the top end of Northern Dale, with tree tufted Tearsall to the left.

In the dale bottom bear right, passing the capped shaft into Tearsall Pipe Caverns on the right. Pass through a stile, bearing right along the waymarked path, through a gap in the wall. There bear left, skirting to the left of another mine. At the next stile, the path forks. Keep left, beside the wall, making for Dalefields Barn. After the second stile, a track is joined. Pass the barn, soon descending sharply into the top of Wensley Dale. In the dale bottom is a totem pole of waymarks. (Here those who took the short cut mentioned earlier would rejoin the walk.)

Follow the track out of the dale up to Wensley. At the first houses, go through a stile on the right, following a tarred footpath through the fields to the main road. Cross the road and go through the stile opposite, signed to Stanton Moor and Birchover. This goes up a driveway, but it is a public footpath. Skirt to the right of the house to reach a green lane. Just beyond the ruined barn, go through a stile on the right, by a gate. Go down the field, heading for a point midway down the left hand boundary where there is a stile. Continue on the same alignment to a stile in the bottom corner of the next field and so enter woodland.

Follow the forest ride through the pines, descending steeply to cross the Clough Wood Brook. Beyond the brook the rough track climbs through new plantation, part of the screening surrounding Enthoven's works. The track soon reaches the road. Just before the road, turn right, following a path beside the fence, through the trees. This avoids road walking, eventually emerging just by the narrow bridge over the Clough Wood Brook. Cross the bridge and go along the road to the T junction by the post office and the Three Stags Heads. Turn left to reach Darley Bridge and the Square and Compass.

Rowsley and Calton Lees

Length of walk: 5 miles.
Start/finish: Peacock Hotel, Rowsley. Daily buses from Matlock. Car
parking at Station Yard, just off A6.
Terrain: Obvious tracks and paths through woodland and parkland. A
lengthy, steady ascent at the start but a long level stretch to finish.

This walk offers a unique opportunity to pass through Rutland to Devonshire
without leaving Derbyshire. From the Peacock, go right, up Church Lane,
passing the village well on the left. Rowsley once belonged to the Duke of
Rutland and the estate still has a considerable influence over the village.
Continue up past the church of St. Katherine's to the last houses in Rowsley.
Nearby is a seat which offers a respite from the climb, though you shouldn't
really need it at this stage. The view down the valley is a good one though.

Soon the lane deteriorates into a rough track, though this was once the main
road to Bakewell. At the trees the lane turns sharp right and climbs more
steeply, soon reaching a fork. Follow the left hand path, passing a metal barrier.
The way is now almost level, though frequently muddy, through Bouns Corner
Wood. There is a short rise and the track emerges from the wood. Here there is
a good view to the left, across to Pic Tor and Stanton Moor. At the T junction
of tracks, go straight on, descending and soon reaching another metal barrier at
a three way junction. Bakewell can be seen ahead.

Take the right hand route, signposted as a bridleway. This enters trees again
and climbs steadily and easily through Rowsleymoor Wood as a broad track.
This is no monoculture of spruce, but a fine mixed deciduous woodland, a
haven for bird and animal life. Soon another track is reached, trailing in
from the right. Bear left here, but in about 100 yards, at the Haddon Estate
sign, turn right and ascend quite sharply, still on a broad rough track. Now
the trees are pines, but well spaced and old.

The track levels out and soon runs alongside a wall, which marks the
boundary between the Duke of Rutland's estates and those of the Dukes of
Devonshire. At a gateway, by a viewpoint, the path leaves Rutland and
enters Devonshire. Continue along the now level path, through a patchwork

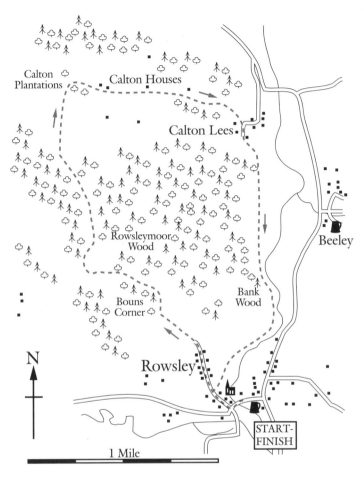

of spruce, following a powerline. The path reaches a gate, where a waymark directs you to the right, through the trees, to a ladder stile. Here, at last, you reach open country, the back of Chatsworth Park. There is a grand view across the parkland to the Russian Cottage and over to the Eastmoors.

The path splits three ways. Take the one which is not waymarked, but which bears left, an obvious worn path which soon begins to descend. Follow the path down into a small valley, passing the troughs on the left and a couple of waymarks, soon reaching the wall surrounding Calton Plantation. Crowded in by the hillside on the left and the trees on the right, the path soon finds a gap in the latter. Cross the bridge over the Calton Brook, go through the gate and turn right, following the plantation wall again. In about 200 yards, turn right, through a gate and follow the track through the delightful little hamlet of Calton Houses.

Where the track emerges from the buildings, there is a view down the valley and a sharp right and left sweep to the valley floor. Enjoy an easy stroll, with the Calton Brook burbling away on the right. This part of the walk seems to be alive with pheasants. Soon the estate village of Calton Lees is reached. At the junction, by the entrance gates, there are two seats. If there are demands for refreshments a 200 yard stroll further along the now tarred road will soon bring you to the Chatsworth Garden Centre. Otherwise, turn right, dipping to cross the culverted stream, then rising again to pass Calton Lees Farm, which sells goats' milk. Look out for a stile on the left, signposted to Rowsley.

Follow the wall on the left, with a good view over the valley to Beeley village and the moors beyond. Soon the path passes through a gateway on the left, then bears right, descending to the valley bottom. Pass through an invariably muddy gateway and then straight across a couple of large fields on an obvious path. In the second field the path comes close to  the River Derwent, only to leave it again, heading for a stile and blocked up gateway. Here you leave Devonshire and re-enter Rutland territory. The path makes its way muddily through scrubby trees before emerging into the open again. Follow the wall on the right, soon coming alongside the river again. A broad, muddy track is followed. This soon becomes a walled and hedged lane, with little chance to escape the mud. The track passes under a bridge carrying the former railway line and there is a glimpse of the fine viaduct to the left. Beyond the bridge the track emerges into Church Lane again. Turn left to reach the main road, the bus stop, the car park, Caudwells Mill and the promise of refreshment.

Winster and Robin Hood's Stride

Length of walk: 4 miles.
Start/finish: Winster Market Hall in the centre of the village. Monday to Saturday buses from Matlock. Car parking just beyond the church (or near the school on Sundays only).
Terrain: Mainly good paths and tracks with only one steep descent. However, Robin Hood's Stride is a rough rocky tor.

From the Market Hall, go along the main street past the post office before turning left up West Bank. Almost at once cross the road and go along a narrow alleyway which leads into the churchyard. Keep left where the path forks, following the edge of the churchyard to a stile. Pass through the stile into the parkland surrounding Oddo House.

Follow the obvious path through the parkland and through a series of stiles, which are unusual, being composed of large lumps of limestone. There is a widening view to the right. On a clear day Robin Hood's Stride is very prominent, but the view will extend to the pointed top of Wardlow Hay Cop and beyond that to Kinder Scout and the mast crowning Sir William Hill. Soon the main road is reached. Cross with care and go over a stile opposite. Continue through fields, with the limestone lump of Grey Tor rising to the left. After the fourth stile from the road the path bears right to a signposted stile where the Portway is joined.

This ancient route dates back to Roman times and maybe even earlier. It is now a quiet track. Turn right at the signpost and go straight on at the adjacent cross 'roads'. An easy stroll along this green lane soon takes you to Elton Cross. When the Portway was the main road there was a pub here. Go across the road and down Dudwood Lane which descends steeply, soon passing the little hamlet of Dudwood.

At the bottom of the hill go straight on, over a stile and up the broad track towards Robin Hood's Stride, which now towers above. From this angle it is clear how it got its other name of Mock Beggars Hall, for the two

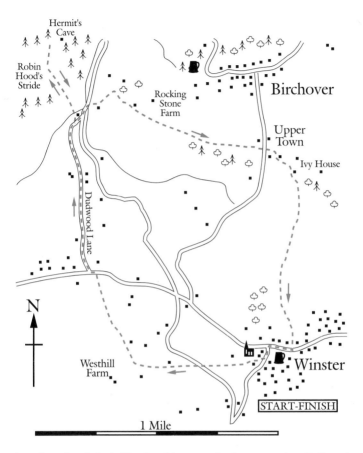

pinnacles of rock look like the chimneys of a large mansion. Follow the track up to the Stride and what is almost certainly a compulsory stop for a scramble. Unless you are an experienced climber, neither of the two towers should be attempted, but there are some good scrambly routes on the lower rocks and the view from the area between the two pinnacles is superb.

On leaving the Stride, don't go back down the track, but instead go through the gate towards Cratcliffe Tor which lies across a flat field. In this field are the remains of a pallisaded encampment, well seen from the Stride. To the left can be seen the few remaining standing stones of Harthill Moor stone

31

circle. At the far end of the field, pass through a stile and then go right, scrambling amongst the rocks and trees to locate the hermit's cave. The carved crucifix and the hermit's sleeping platform can be seen, as well as the ingenious grooves in the rock wall, by which water was fed to the cave.

Leave the cave by the steeply descending path which soon reaches the edge of the wood at a stile. A path follows the edge of the wood back towards the Stride, but then goes left, over a stile into the field. Follow the track back down the field to reach Dudwood Lane again. Go left and left again at the main road, taking great care as there is no footway or verge and there are always parked cars. About 150 yds along the road, just opposite a milepost, go right, over a stile and back into fields.

A short steep ascent takes you to a stile where you should turn sharp right. Do not follow the more obvious track straight ahead. Almost at once, bear left, following the wall beside the trees to another stile. An obvious path skirts the base of Rocking Stone Tor, passing the ruins of a barn, whose rear wall was hewn into a slab of rock. Pass Rocking Stone Farm on the left and continue ahead, with Birchover village now in view. Winster and Elton can be seen to the right, across the valley.

The path keeps to the edge of the scarp, passing through a series of fields until the little settlement of Upper Town in reached. (Just to the left of the point where the path joins the road, there is a set of stocks; of potential use in the case of recalcitrant offspring.) Cross the road and go up the flight of steps opposite, passing through the yard of Cowley Knoll Farm to reach Clough Lane. Turn right here and follow the lane round the bend where there is a grand view across to Winster.

A little over 100 yds beyond the bend, go right at a footpath sign by a big ash tree. Follow the hedge on the right to a stile and gate, beyond which the land falls away steeply. A freshly made cart track zigzags down the hillside, eventually losing itself in the flatter grassland below. Keep straight on, with a little valley to the right, passing the end of a remnant hedge on the left until a broad path is reached. Follow this towards Winster. The path dips sharply to a stile, beyond which it becomes paved with gritstone. Follow this obvious route through a series of fields, gradually climbing towards the village. For the most part the stiles are obvious and waymarked. Where the path joins a track, continue uphill, via the cattle grid, not the steps. The first houses of Winster are soon reached and the lane emerges in the main street close to the Market Hall and right beside a shop selling ice cream.